Preface:

To begin, I would like to thank you for buying this ebook, and I hope you enjoy reading it as much as I loved scouring an immense amount of shower thoughts to find the ones that I appreciated most.

It was difficult because so many shower thoughts revolve around certain websites, politics or current events. Which, for the most part, just would not connect with most readers. You also hit a point where most shower thoughts are just silly or rehashed versions of ones that you have already read. That said, I persevered and even added some of my own to the book. These are not marked as mine, so hopefully they just blend in.

I decided to put together a collection of my favourite one hundred shower thoughts, because I felt they tend to bring a little joy to me and most other people I know when we read them, and usually they can be hard to find past a group of five or six that are constantly repeated. That was just the simple reason though: everyone wants to create something that people will enjoy.

The other reason shower thoughts drew me in is the crude link to a human mind that they provide. Poetry is a link to the poet, what they saw, what they thought and what they felt. That's what's so beautiful about it. Shower thoughts are similar, except they are just short, unedited snippets of what that mind was thinking at that particular moment. Most people wouldn't even bother sharing these thoughts, and that's what I like about them. We're all crazy, deep down inside, and this is proof.

Brief Introduction:

A shower thought is any thought you ponder on in the shower, or actually anywhere. Most shower thoughts are probably not thought up in the shower, they are popping in to your head when you are daydreaming in class, or dozing off at work. They are just typically associated with the shower. The following are a collection of the good, the bad and the ugliest shower thoughts.

Shower Thoughts 1-5

1. When someone complains about the younger generation, they're really complaining about how bad at parenting their generation was.

2. If a Cuban man has a child with an Icelandic woman, would the children be IceCubes?

3. In professional sports, when the countries Sweden and Denmark play each other, the three letter abbreviations used for the teams are SWE and DEN. The unused letters remaining for each country are DEN and MARK.

4. School is meant to bring new humans up to speed on humanity's progress so far.

5. At a 27MPH top speed, it is illegal for Usain Bolt to run in a school zone.

Shower Thoughts 6-10

6. We use the phrase 'slept like a baby' to describe sleeping very well, but babies are notorious for waking up in the middle of the night, crying.

7. If you're an Agnostic, then starting a prayer with "To Whom It May Concern" would probably be the most effective technique.

8. Let's give thanks to all the people that died a long time ago working out which plants were edible and which were not.

9. The iconic alien is to us, as we are to apes; small, pale, big headed and with unfathomable technology. We even abduct them for medical experiments.

10. During childhood, jokes about the genital regions are considered adult content, but when we become adults those same jokes are considered childish.

Shower Thoughts 11-15

11. The fact that there is a Highway to Hell, and only a Stairway to Heaven says a lot about the expected traffic to both.

12. We say hair when we are referring to a lot of them, but hairs when we are referring to only a few of them.

13. Humans are the only animals intelligent enough to call each other stupid.

14. Nasa is able to receive data from craft 4.67 billion miles away, but my phone loses wifi coverage if I take it into the kitchen.

15. Every cell in a human body knows how to replicate DNA, but we're not in on it, so we have to study it.

Shower Thoughts 16-20

16. There's a little under 500 billionaires on the planet, and not one of those losers has chosen to become Batman.

17. The first person to try a hot pepper probably thought something very dangerous was happening to them.

18. If you're watching a sunset, someone on the other side of the world is watching the same sun rise.

19. An elderly couple in a coffee shop in the future may one day hear Baby by Justin Bieber play and exclaim "look honey, they're playing our song"

20. Taking candy from a baby is actually a very responsible thing to do.

Shower Thoughts 21-25

21. If most people were stranded on an island with a fully functioning plane and runway, they would still not be able to escape that island.

22. Whilst it's hard to win an argument with a smart person, it's damn near impossible to win an argument with a stupid person.

23. Companies that sell pens or lighters must make a lot of money off of people losing them and buying replacements.

24. The Milky Way Galaxy could well be the Galaxy with the most milk in it.

25. Queue is pronounced the same as the letter Q making 80% of the letters used in spelling it obsolete.

Shower Thoughts 26-30

26. If we had no eyes then we would be unaware of the existence of colour. What if we are missing an entire aspect of everything because we do not have the organ to detect it.

27. Caterpillars have mastered beauty sleep.

28. I wonder if my cat thinks the pizza delivery guy is my owner because HE gives ME food.

29. Scooby-Doo has taught us that the real monsters always turn out to be humans.

30. When you die in a dream, you wake up; this is because you don't know what happens next.

Shower Thoughts 31-35

31. Stereotypically, Old people drive like they have all the time in the world, and Young people drive like their time is extremely limited.

32. iPhone chargers should be called Apple Juice

33. The phrase "love you to the moon and back" is pretty insulting to an astronomer. "Out of all the objects in the universe, you chose the one closest to Earth?"

34. Every single decision you have made in your life, has led you to this moment now, to read this sentence.

35. Your shadow is confirmation that light has travelled nearly 93 million miles unobstructed, only to be deprived of reaching the ground in the final few feet thanks to you.

Shower Thoughts 36-40

36. Apple should have called their store "The Orchard"

37. The planet Mars is populated entirely by Robots.

38. Life on Earth is the cosmic equivalent of what happens when you don't store things in a cool, dry place.

39. Fat Chance and Slim Chance mean exactly the same thing.

40. Rubix Cubes are little life lessons. A problem seems difficult and complex at first, but as you work at it you start slowly solving it, bit by bit, making it easier as you go along. Until you realise that it was never difficult, it just took many small, easy steps. The problem was trying to solve it in one big difficult step.

Shower Thoughts 41-45

41. The tallest person on Earth has been the height of every other person on Earth at some point in their life.

42. When somebody has gotten sunburnt, they've actually been burnt by an object 93 million miles away.

43. When you drink alcohol, you are just borrowing happiness from tomorrow.

44. Since China hosts a billion people, one-in-a-million things happen one thousand times a day to people there.

45. Whilst you aren't allowed to use steroids to enhance performance in sports, you are encourage to use make-up to enhance beauty in beauty pageants.

Shower Thoughts 46-50

46. Your age is just the number of laps you have done around a giant fireball in the middle of the solar system.

47. In Japan, radiation creates monsters. In America, radiation creates superheroes.

48. The reason that things seem to be better made in the past, is that all the badly made stuff didn't survive until today for you to see it, so you are only seeing the highest quality items from the past.

49. Thanks to the internet, I have probably seen more naked people than all of my ancestors combined.

50. Humans built an atomic bomb twenty years before they managed colour television.

Shower Thoughts 51-55

51. If you rip a hole in a net, there's actually fewer holes in it than there was before.

52. The letter X seems to be far more commonly used in Maths than it is in English.

53. Nothing is ever on fire, it is the fire that is on those things.

54. History classes are only going to get longer and harder as time goes on.

55. If you went back in time to kill Hitler when he was a baby, then you would just be some horrible person that killed a baby, and no one would ever know what you stopped from happening.

Shower Thoughts 56-60

56. If there is an example of the perfect crime, you will never hear about it.

57. Only the day that you are born, and the day that you die on will ever be less than 24 hours long in length.

58. Newborns are always crying because any minor discomfort is literally one of the worst things they have ever experienced.

59. The word indescribable means that it's now possible to describe everything.

60. The sole objective in Golf is to play the least amount of Golf.

Shower Thoughts 61-65

61. If you mounted Garbage trucks with Cameras, you could update Google Maps street view weekly.

62. Most peoples first word of the year is "Happy"

63. At some point all of your best friends were strangers.

64. Disney Land is the greatest Human Trap that a Mouse has ever made.

65. Wasps and Bees sting to prevent their nests being destroyed, but the fact that they do sting is the primary reason humans destroy their nests.

Shower Thoughts 66-70

66. Art is how we decorate space; Music is how we decorate time.

67. Clapping is just hitting yourself because you like something.

68. A mile a minute sounds faster than 60 MPH.

69. The person that would proofread Adolf Hitlers speeches, was a grammar Nazi.

70. If the oldest person on earth is 116 years old, then 117 years ago there was an entirely different set of people on the earth.

Shower Thoughts 71-75

71. What if every country has ninjas, but we only hear about the Japanese ones because they're rubbish?

72. Santa Claus probably regrets giving coal to naughty kids now that global warming is threatening his habitat.

73. Every day someone on Earth unknowingly does the biggest poop in the world for that day.

74. April Fools Day is the only day of the year where people critically evaluate every news article before accepting them as true.

75. I wonder if I Have ever been bitten by a mosquito that's descended from one that I failed to kill previously.

Shower Thoughts 76-80

76. If you could literally be bored to death, the world would be a much more interesting place.

77. The future will only look futuristic because we will be trying to make it look the way we expect it to look; futuristic.

78. Bullets only do their job after they're fired.

79. In English, both the letters C and X are almost redundant. The soft C sounds like an S, and the hard C sounds like a K, meaning you could just use those letters instead. The soft X sounds like a Z and the hard X sounds like 'EKS' so again could be made just by using those combinations.

80. You never know how many people you dislike until it comes to naming your child.

Shower Thoughts 81-85

81. If you believe in reincarnation then your tombstone should say B.R.B (Be Right Back) instead of R.I.P (Rest In Peace)

82. Zero is plural, whereas One is singular.

83. I don't think I Have ever heard a car alarm go off and thought "oh shit, someone's car is being stolen, I should probably call the police"

84. If you didn't know what "Waterboarding" or "Guantanamo Bay" meant, then the phrase "Waterboarding at Guantanamo Bay" sounds really cool.

85. Since most people are buried in suits, a Zombie Apocalypse would be a formal event.

Shower Thoughts 86-90

86. Cowboys that ride off into the sunset quickly run out of daylight and have to camp just outside of town. Probably should have just stayed put for the night instead of being all dramatic.

87. The first person to ever hear a parrot speak, must have freaked out.

88. If you've stolen pens from a bank, you have technically robbed a bank.

89. Imitating a gun to your own head with your fingers means suicide, but imitating a knife to your own neck is intimidation.

90. USB sounds like a backup plan in case USA fails.

Shower Thoughts 91-95

91. We delay going to bed because we want to stay awake longer, but then we delay getting up because we want to sleep longer. We have created our own paradox that will constantly frustrate us.

92. Trying to get rich by playing the lottery, is like trying to commit suicide by flying on commercial airlines.

93. A group of Squid should be called a Squad.

94. Despite being an Island, Antarctica doesn't have a south coast. Only one big north coast.

95. We use sex to buy and sell everything, yet we arrest those who buy and sell actual sex.

Shower Thoughts 96-100

96. When a Pregnant Woman swims, she is a human submarine.

97. If Humans could fly, we'd probably consider it exercise and never do it.

98. Maybe it's called Sand because it's between the sea and the land.

99. Going to bed when you're ill and feeling better in the morning is the human equivalent of turning an electrical device off and on again to fix it.

100. Every single person that has ever had a shower has an idea. It is the person who gets out of the shower, dries them self off and does something about the idea that makes a difference.

Afterword:

Thank you so much for reading through to the end, if you enjoyed this then please consider looking through our other books. If you like poetry, you may also enjoy Autumn Verses: A Poetry Collection. Also look out for Winter Verses: A Poetry Collection which will be released soon.

If you have any ideas on future collections or books you would like to see, then please feel free to email us at:
bryant.murrell.publishing@gmail.com

Also feel free to follow us on twitter:
@Bryant_Murrell

Finally, if you did enjoy reading these shower thoughts, then it would be really helpful for us if you left a review. Thank you for taking the time to read this, and even more so if you did follow us or buy one of our other books.